YEAR ZERO OF OUR LORD PEWDIEPIE

In the beginning was the Word—and the Word was with PewDiePie, and the Word was PewDiePie.

Through PewDiePie all things were created; there was nothing that was not created by PewDiePie.

PewDiePie saw that it was all good. And with that, Lord PewDiePie descended from his higher state to enter the Earth realm through an intergalactic portal known as his mom.

THE YEAR TWENTY-FIVE A.P.
(After PewDiePie)

Seeing that the young World was in need of his guidance, the great Lord PewDiePie chose to spread his infinite and bountiful wisdom across all dimensions of the Earth.

Now the fields shall be abundant with great harvests, and your tables shall be laden with his fruit. The vineyards shall drip sweet wine, and your cup shall overfloweth with his magnificent juice.

From henceforth, in the name of the great Lord PewDiePie, a glorious new world shall await all those who bathe in the greatness of this book.

*And it is to be known by every man, woman, and child, that **This Book Loves You**.*

THIS BOOK LOVES YOU

PEWDIEPIE

RAZORBILL
an imprint of
PENGUIN RANDOM HOUSE

THIS BOOK LOVES YOU

PewDiePie

A few years ago, it came to my attention on Twitter that a fan had taken one of my tweets and turned it into a beautiful page design. It was of a quote I had written as a parody of all those many pearls of wisdom that the Internet tries to share with the World. And so, I discovered the importance of my great wisdom, and it was clear to me that the World desperately needed my teachings. But was the World ready for such enlightenment?

(Please don't quote this.)

I must confess that I have never truly understood the purpose of quotes. If I had listened to half the things that I'm told online, I would not be here today. In fact, if I had listened to the Internet, my life would have gone very wrong, very quickly. But still the Internet shouts inspirational words at me: *Happiness, Be Strong, Positivity, Goodness.* Why are strangers taunting me with things I can't have? Who are these sadistic, smug quote-makers?

(Please don't quote this.)

And so, for a laugh, I decided to write a book of inspirational quotes . . . a whole book filled with the wisdom of PewDiePie. I hope, perhaps, that this book will motivate, encourage, and energize all of you into living your lives to the fullest? Maybe it will help you to view those inspirational quotes you see on the Internet with a more skeptical eye? Or perhaps you'll just find it a welcome distraction from that difficult bowel movement you're experiencing as you read?

(Please don't quote this.)

I hope you enjoy it, but don't try to eat it.
The lasagna version will be released in the near future.

This book was ghostwritten by Edgar.

NEVER
that
BEAUT

FORGET

you're

IFUL...

compared to
A FISH.
LIFE IS ALL
ABOUT
perspective!

MONEY
CAN'T BUY YOU
HAPPINESS

BUT IT BUYS YOU
ALL THE THINGS
YOU DON'T HAVE,
EVEN FRIENDS.

The more

you give,

the more

you lose.

NEVER
GIVE UP
UNLESS YOU'VE TRIED
AT LEAST 3 TIMES
COS
THEN IT'S JUST
IMPOSSIBLE

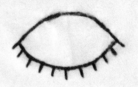

DON'T BE
AFRAID TO SAY
HOW U FEEL,
BECAUSE
NO ONE IS
GOING TO
CARE
ANYWAY.

Roses are Red

Violets are Blue

Eat a .

RUNNING AWAY FROM YOUR PROBLEMS WON'T MAKE YOU SKINNY.

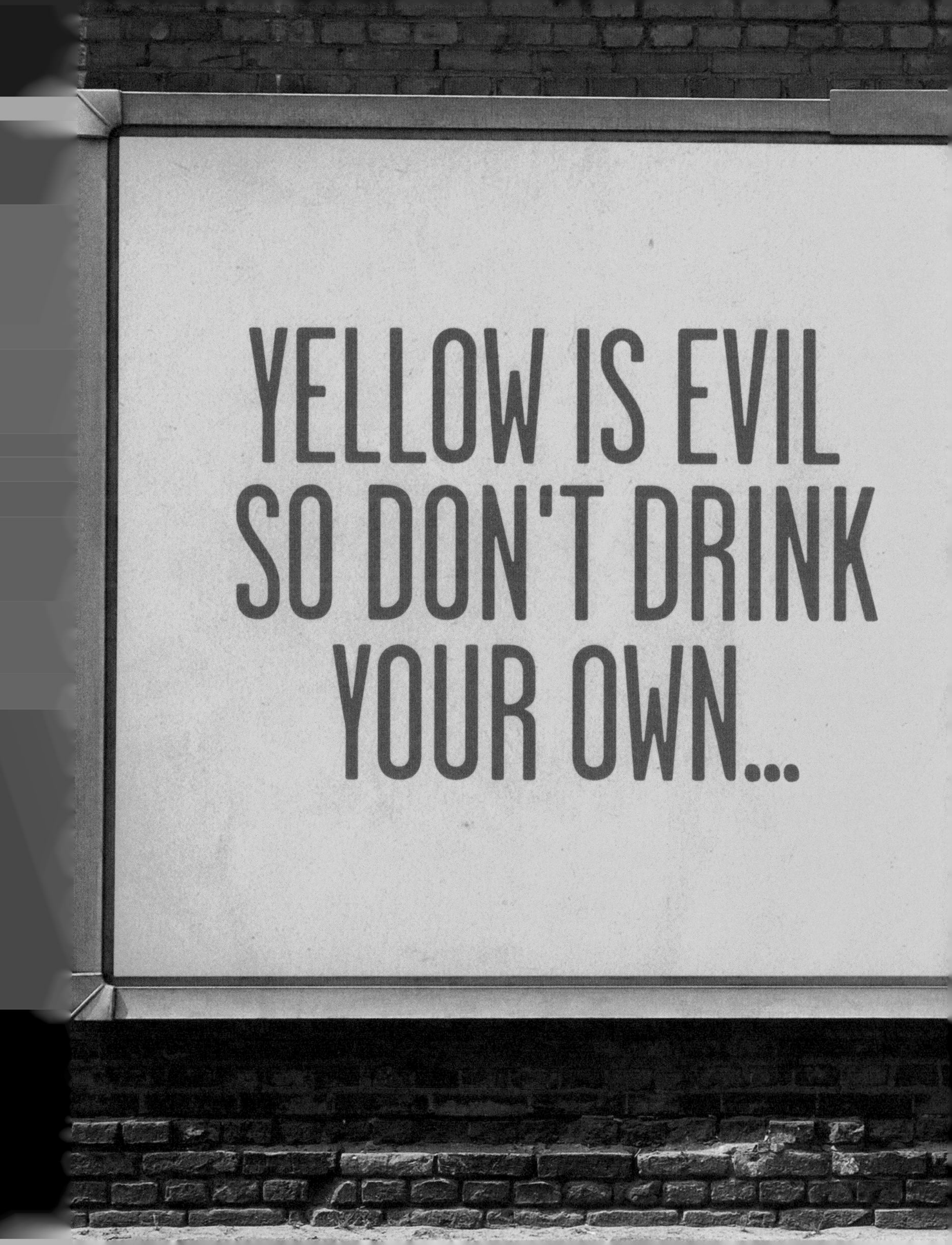
YELLOW IS EVIL
SO DON'T DRINK
YOUR OWN...

IF YOU CAN
FIGHT
YOUR WAY OUT
★★★★ **OF A** ★★★★
SITUATION

Things ~~can~~ WILL always get worse.

TO FLY, YOU MUST GET RID OF THE THINGS THAT WEIGH YOU DOWN.

THIS IS WHY ALL YOUR FRIENDS LEFT YOU.

NOTHING IN LIFE COMES EASY

SO WHY DO YOU EXPECT SOMETHING OUT OF A QUOTE

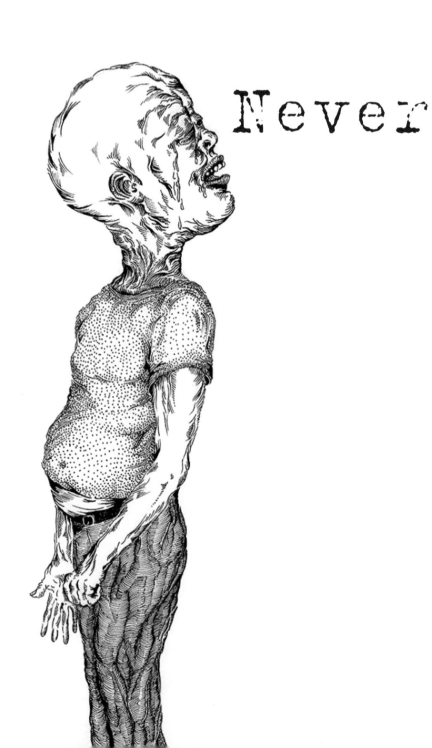

Never

look back.

If life doesn't go right

take a left...

DON'T KILL ANYONE. PEOPLE DIE IF THEY GET KILLED

Everyone is entitled
to their own opinion

F

even though

THEY'RE UCKING WRONG!!

LIFE IS ABOUT LISTENING TO QUOTES THAT RELATE TO YOU, SO YOU CAN FEEL MOMENTARILY BETTER ABOUT YOURSELF.

HERE'S A PICTURE OF A ....

DUCK

YOUR PET
ONLY LOVES
YOU BECAUSE
YOU GIVE
IT FOOD.

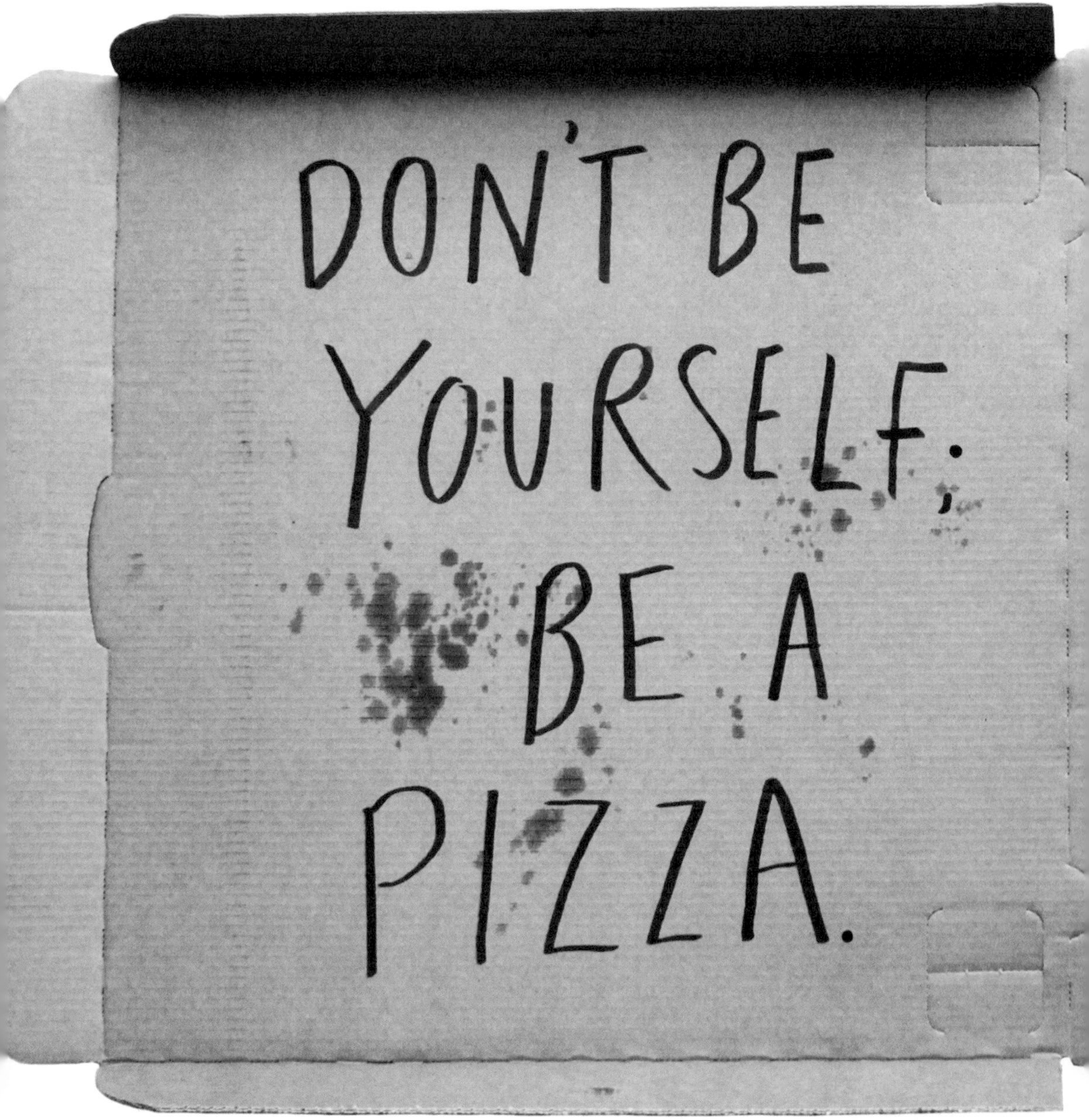
DON'T BE
YOURSELF;
BE A
PIZZA.

Don't be a Bitch.

IT'S NEVER TOO LATE TO GIVE UP.

Don't
sugar coat
everything . . .

you'll get
diabetes.

Impossible is nothing.
Doing nothing is easy.

So do nothing!!

DON'T SELL YOURSELF SHORT . . .

UNLESS YOU NEED
QUICK MONEY.

HEY, I'M NOT JUDGING.

LET'S
FACE IT,
YOU'LL
NEVER
BE AS
COOL
AS THIS.

IF YOU EVER TAKE ADVICE

FROM A DUCK,

REMEMBER:

DON'T.

DUCKS

CAN'T TALK.

YOU'RE PROBABLY ON DRUGS.

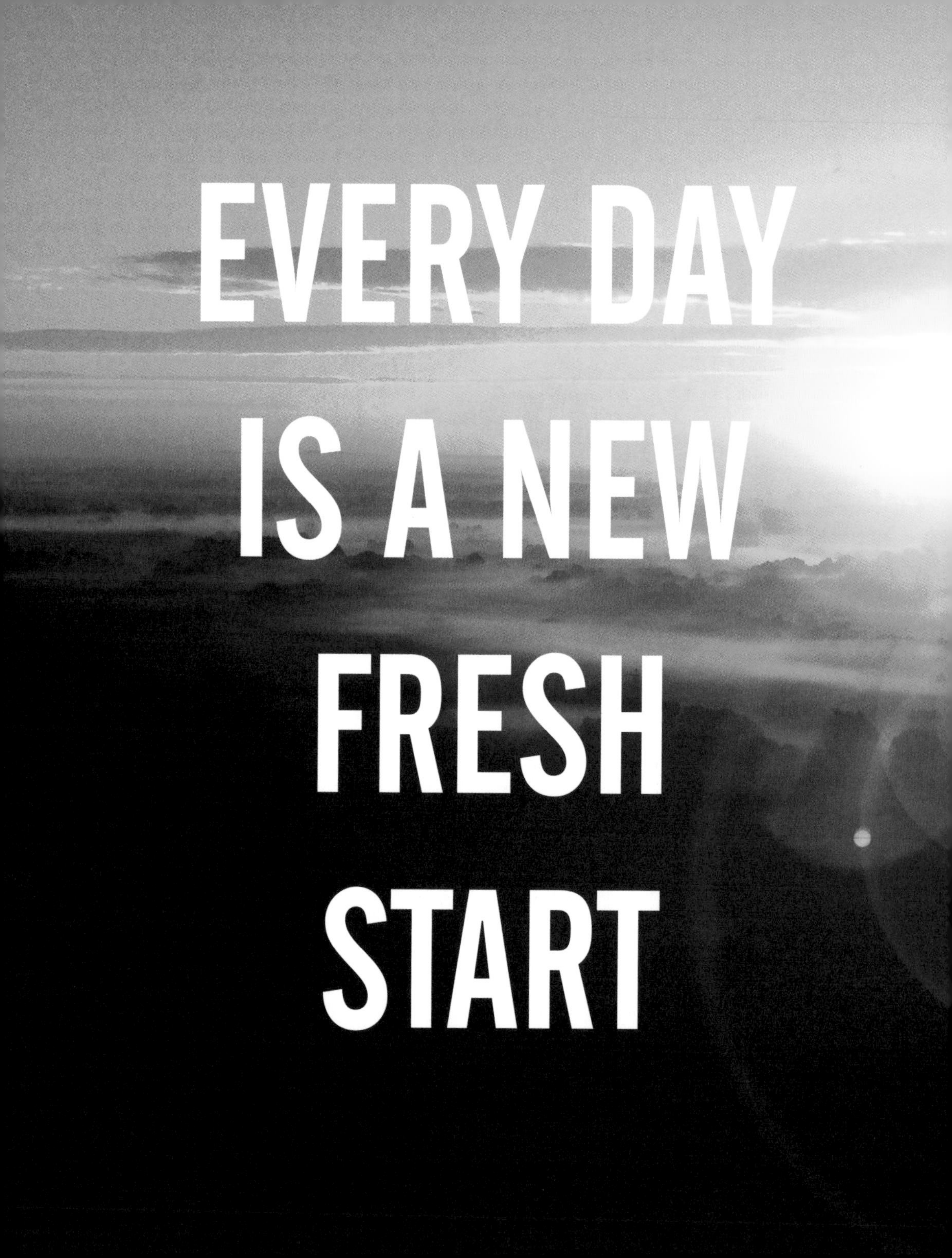
EVERY DAY
IS A NEW
FRESH
START

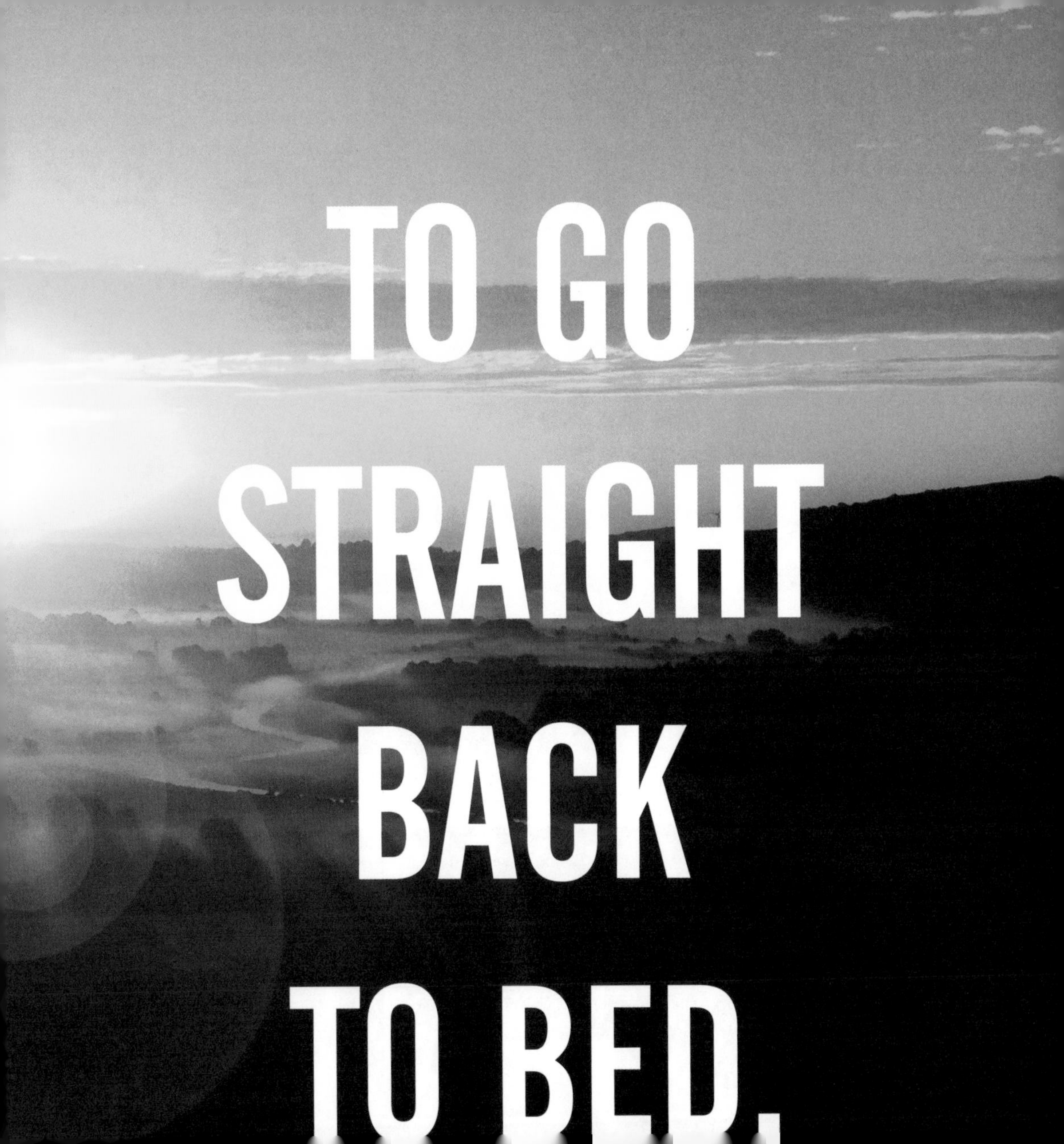
TO GO
STRAIGHT
BACK
TO BED.

IF YOU EVER
FEEL SAD,
JUST REMEMBER:
EVEN UNICORNS
PROBABLY HAVE
DIARRHEA EVERY
ONCE IN A WHILE.

YOU CAN'T WIN THE RACE

~~BY NOT TRYING~~

by cutting off their legs.

MONDAY IS COMING!

LOADING . . .

Running Out
Of Money
DOESN'T COUNT
as EXERCISE.

Without WINTER, you can't fully appreciate the beauty of SUMMER.

Without you, I can appreciate so many things.

IF YOU EVER DON'T FEEL SPECIAL, JUST REMEMBER: YOU'RE THE... #1 SPERM!

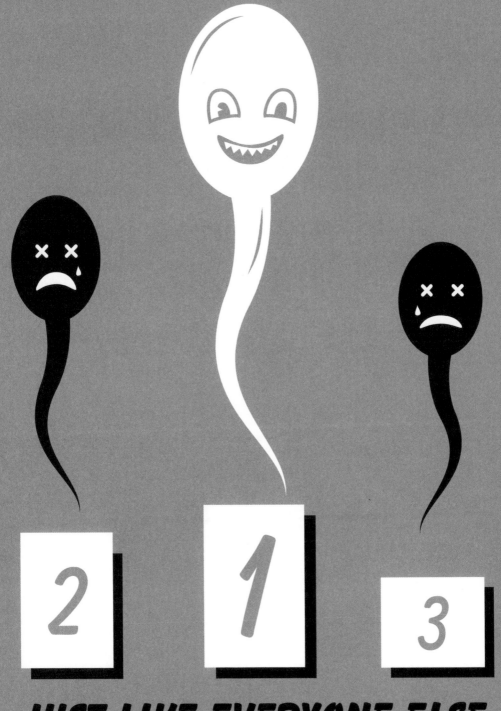

DO YOU REMEMBER ALL THE EMBARRASSING MOMENTS YOU'VE HAD? DON'T WORRY, I'LL REMIND YOU.
– BRAIN

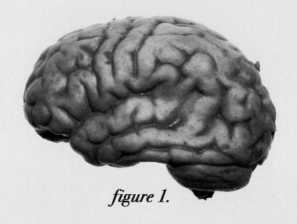

figure 1.

YOU CAN NEVER FAIL IF YOU NEVER TRY

SO WHY BOTHER.

THERE CAN'T BE WINNERS WITHOUT LOSERS

SO REALLY YOU'RE DOING THE WORLD A FAVOR.

smile*

*It makes you look like a psychopath.

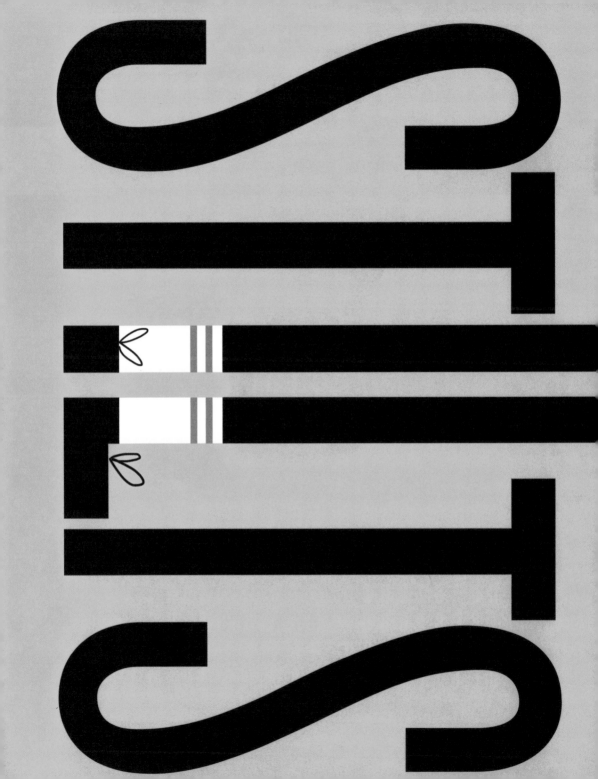

IF YOU
EVER FEEL
DOWN . . .

JUST REMEMBER:
NO ONE ELSE IS
ABOVE YOU

IF YOU WEAR

IF YOU'RE ROUND, YOU MIGHT NOT BE IN SHAPE

BUT AT LEAST YOU ARE A SHAPE.

Don't waste time loving someone who doesn't love you back.

Love ducks.

Ducks always love you back.

HATERS
GONNA
HATE

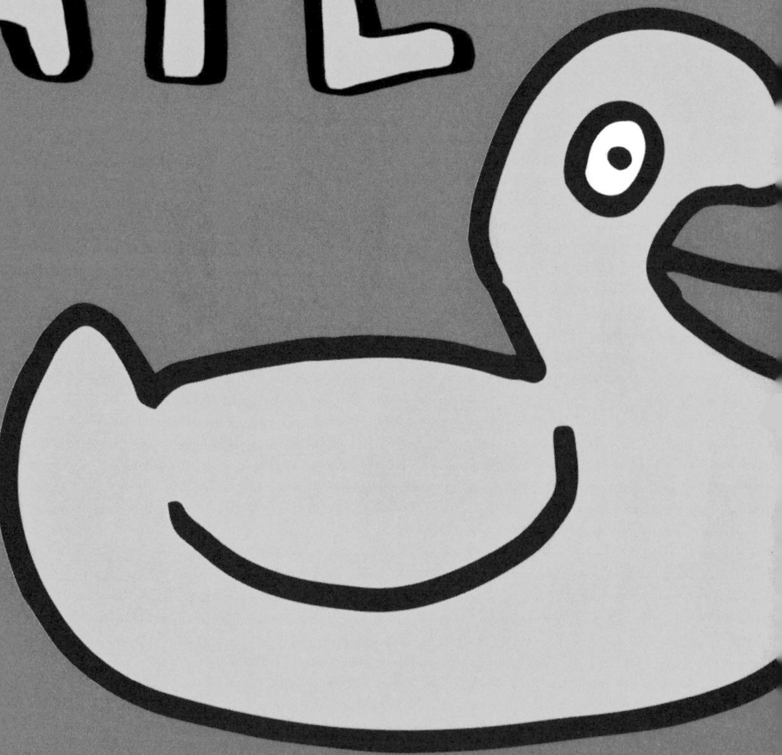

THEY SAY LOVE IS BLIND.

IT'S EITHER THAT OR YOU'LL HAVE TO DATE A BLIND PERSON.

LIFE IS A DEATH SENTENCE AND YOU SHOULD RESENT YOUR PARENTS.

———

Quotes are the most
important thing in
the universe, and you
should always take
them to heart.

———

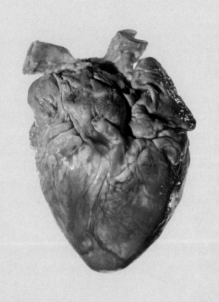

Backflipping constantly is a great way to

If someone hates your guts

feed them to them.

If someone loves your guts

they're probably a zombie.

The Secret to a Happy Life is:

P.T.O. →

YOU SERIOUSLY EXPECTED TO FIND IT IN THIS BOOK? HAHAHA

JUST BECAUSE YOU HAVE AN OPINION

DOESN'T MEAN ANYONE HAS TO GIVE A DUCK.

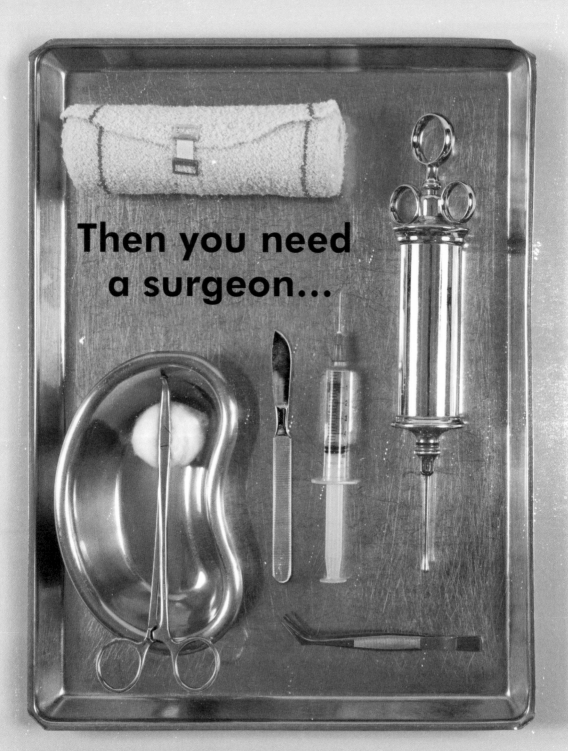

Life without nipples would be pointless.
— Duck

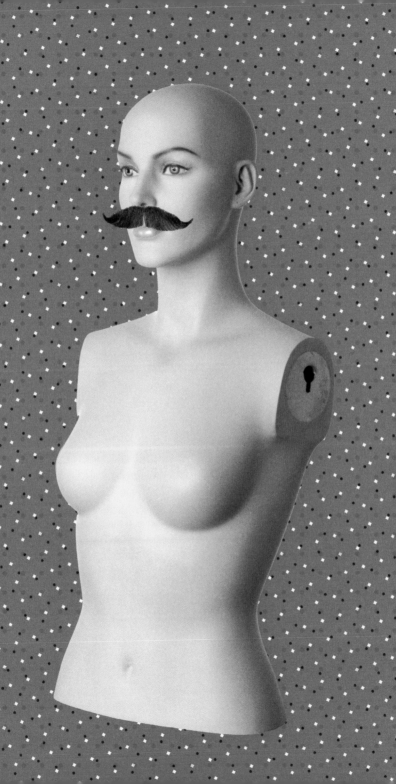

WITHOUT
NIPPLES,
BOOBS
WOULD
JUST BE

BUTT CHEEKS THAT DON'T POOP.

*Except that awkward emo phase you went through.

Hide your tears;
pretend you are ok.
Crying in the shower
camouflages them away.

IF YOU CAN'T AFFORD TO BUY THIS BOOK

OPTION 1: DID YOU STEAL IT?

OPTION 2: SELL YOUR KIDNEY?

OPTION 3: OFFER YOUR SOUL?

DON'T BE A SALAD. BE THE BEST GODDAMN BROCCOLI YOU COULD EVER BE.

Duck
loves
you
THIS
much.

YOU CAN NEVER
BE HUNGOVER
IF YOU ARE
DRUNKS
ALL THE TIMESZS.

THERE'S ALWAYS A NEW DAY TOMORROW

— SHERLOCK

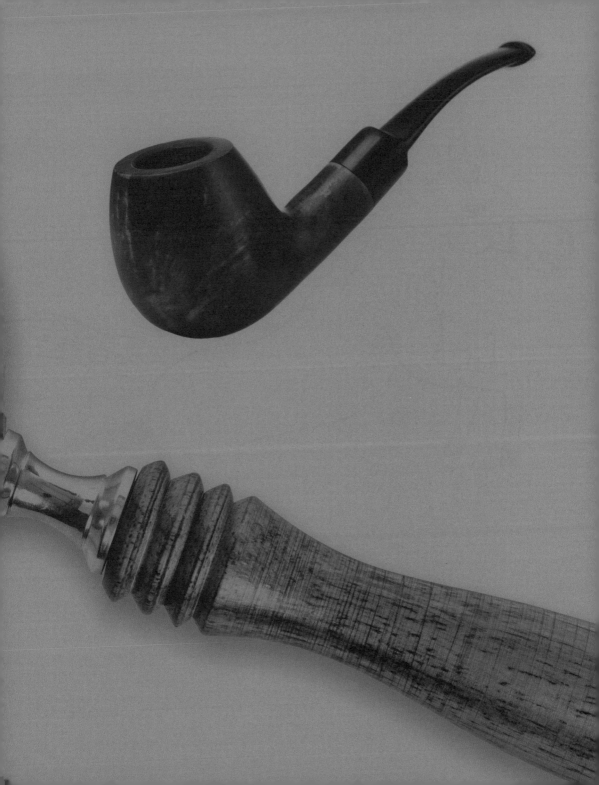

DON'T BE SOMETHING YOU'RE NOT.
UNLESS YOU CAN BE A FABULOUS UNICORN.
ALWAYS BE A FABULOUS UNICORN.

Success is never an accident,
which is why it will never happen to you.

If you can't beat 'em, eat 'em.

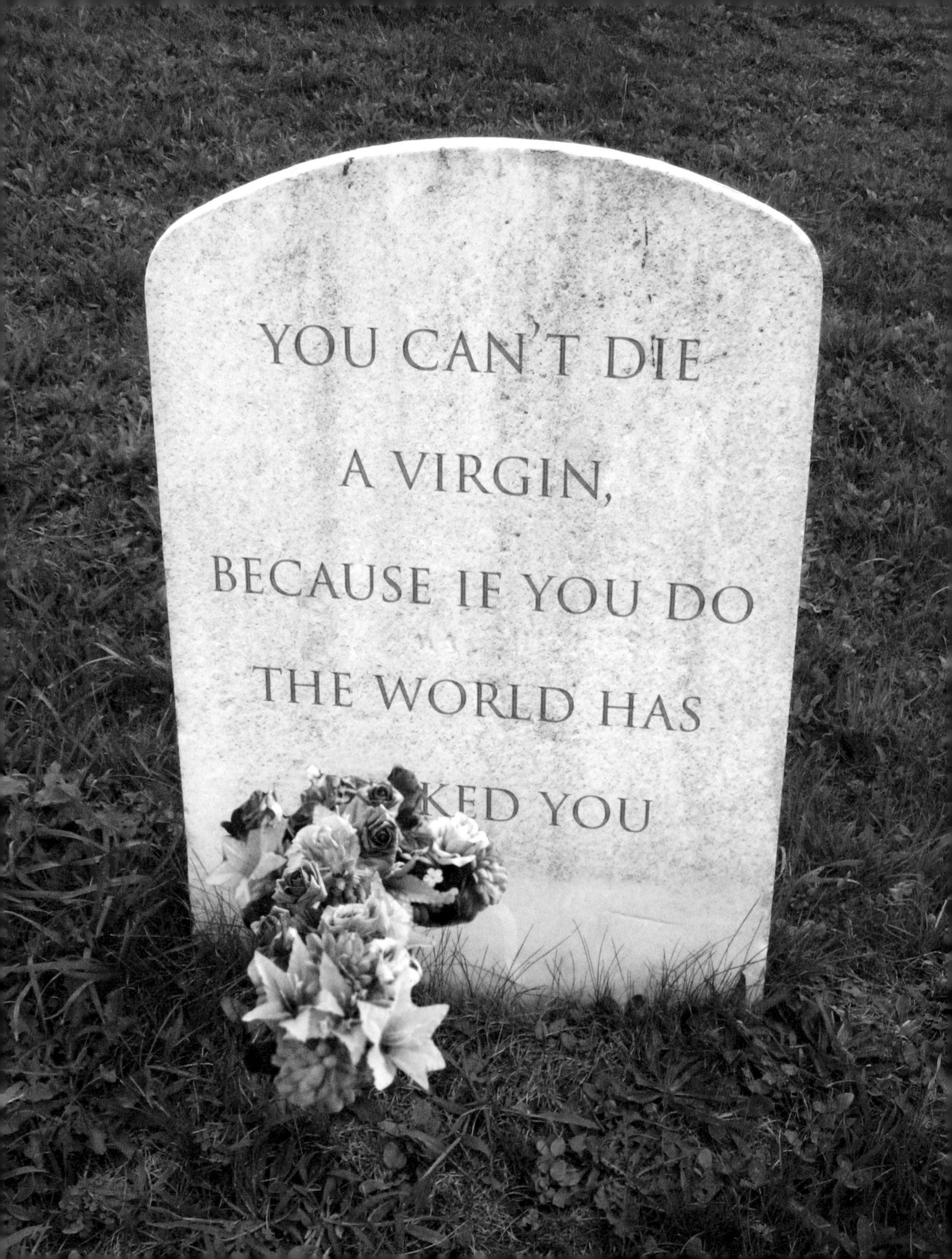
YOU CAN'T DIE
A VIRGIN,
BECAUSE IF YOU DO
THE WORLD HAS
KED YOU

EVERYTHING HAPPENS FOR A REASON.
YES, EVEN THAT AWKWARD RASH YOU HAVE.

MONDAY	TUESDAY	WEDNESDAY	THUR
	5	6	7
11	12 EVERY	13 DAY	14
18	19	20	21
25 BLOODY	HELL	27	28 H MA

	FRIDAY	SATURDAY	SUNDAY
	1 EVERY	**2** DAY	**3** IS A
	8 SECOND	**9** CHAN	**10** CE.
	15 YOU	**16** STILL	**17** FAIL.
	22	**23**	**24**
	29 CHANCES	**30** DO YOU	**31** NEED

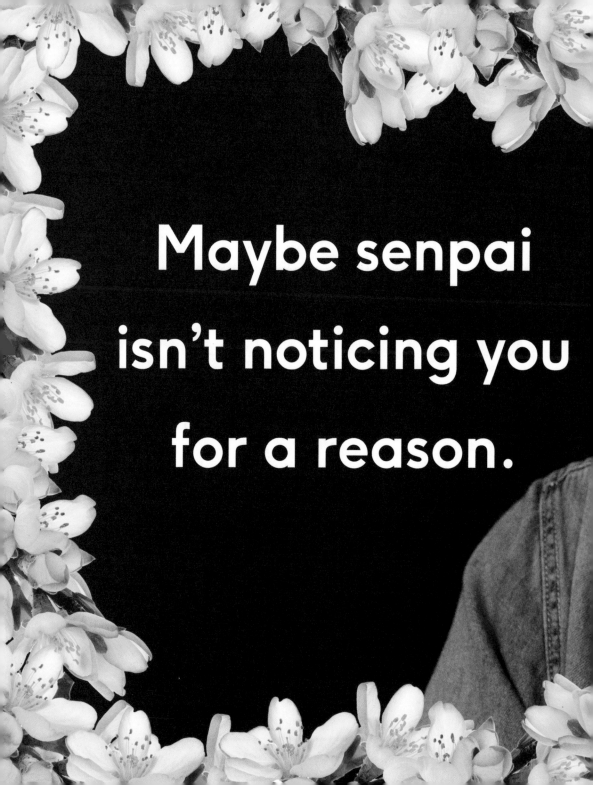

HOW TO BE THE BEST FLAWLESS LAWYER STEP TOP STEP

DO OR DON'T

NEVER EVER DO ANYTHING

YOU'RE WELCOME

If life sucks, get a straw and show life who's boss.

TREAT PEOPLE WHO
BELIEVE IN KARMA BADLY.
THEY OBVIOUSLY HAD
IT COMING.

YOU'RE NOT BAD

EVERYONE ELSE IS JUST SO MUCH BETTER

I prayed for beauty...
it worked.

Don't you forget about me.*

*Cos if you do I'll burn your f@%king house down.

BE NICE TO

THIS MONEY

MAYBE ONE DAY

PEOPLE

LOVES YOU

PEWDIEPIE

Unless you have a face tattoo.

Then you are screwed for life.

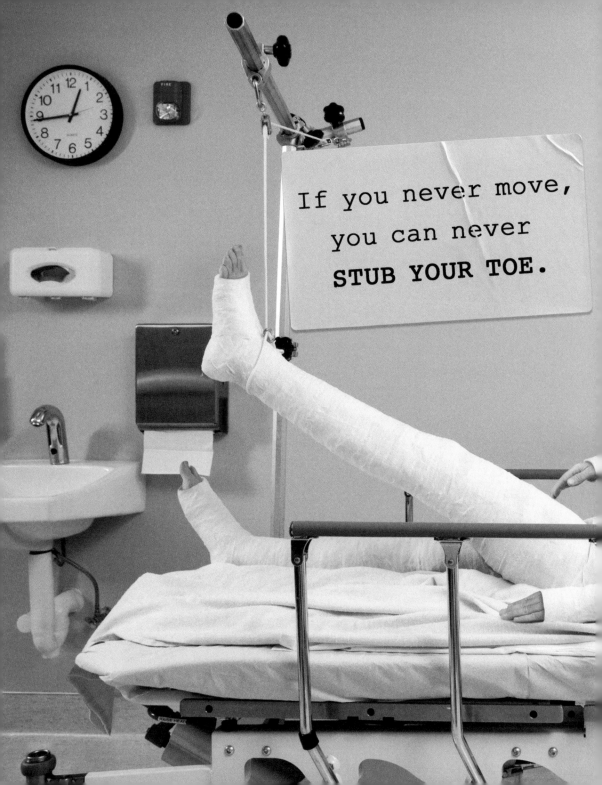

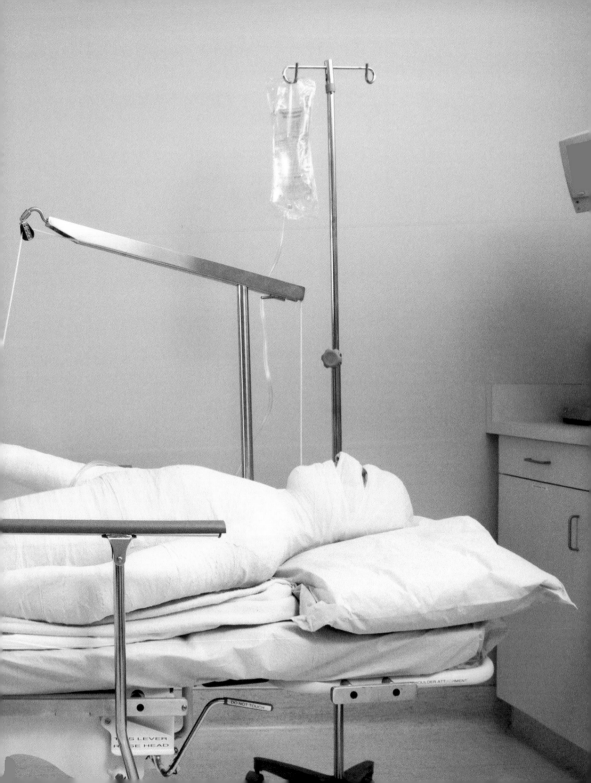

Embrace

your

missteak.

You can't make everyone happy.

So focus on making yourself happy so that maybe one day your happiness will evolve and EAT EVERYONE.

Don't listen to haters.

Live your life the way
you want to live it.

It's important to love yourself.

Because no one else does.

To PewDiePie
love you lots
PewDiePie xxx

NOW ROCK BOTTOM

KEEP YOUR FRIENDS CLOSE

BUT YOUR ENEMIES CLOSER

UNLESS YOU DON'T HAVE ANY FRIENDS

THEN JUST SIT IN A CORNER AND CRY

IF YOU DON'T WIN, YOU LOSE . . .

Just checking to see if you knew.

WHAT DOESN'T KILL YOU

MAKES
YOU
STRONG
ER.

YOU MAY NOT BE STRONG.
YOU MAY NOT BE GOOD ENOUGH.
YOU MAY NEVER EVEN
BE A DECENT PERSON.

I FORGET THE REST...

PewDiePie say:

Don't give up, because if you do, you're seriously such a (_____).

Never give up on those dreams of yours...and stuff.

NEVER, NEVER GIVE UP

COMPLAIN.

DEMAND TO SEE
A MANAGER.
GET
LIFE FIRED
AND RUIN LIFE'S LIFE.
REALIZE YOUR LIFE
IS NOW EMPTY.

DON'T WO
YOUR PI
IF YOU EN
TOMORRO
ALL B

RRY ABOUT
OBLEMS.
UP DEAD
, THEY'LL
GONE.

-DUCK

GIVE A MAN A FISH AND YOU FEED HIM FEED HIM FOR A DAY. BECOME A FISH AND BE HIS L♥VER 4 LIFE.

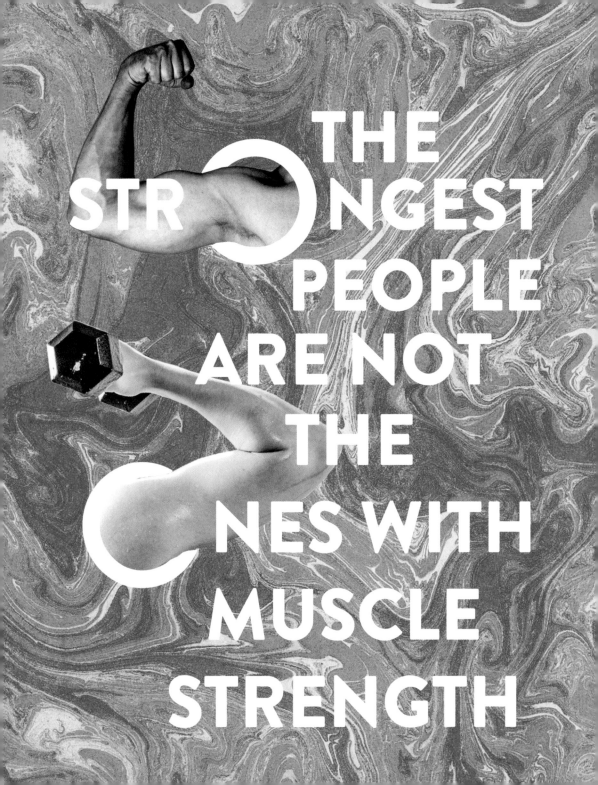

THE STRONGEST PEOPLE ARE NOT THE ONES WITH MUSCLE STRENGTH

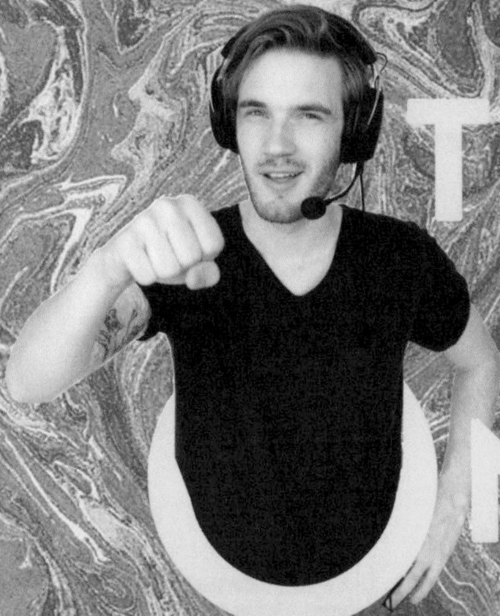

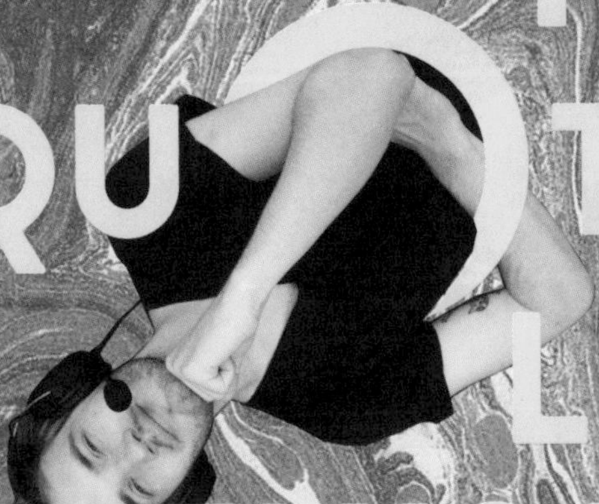

THEY'RE THE ONES THAT NEED QUOTES LIKE THIS TO PULL THROUGH.

DON'T USE TAMPONS IF YOU'RE A BOY

-A Wise Man

EVERY SECOND
YOU'RE CLOSER
TO OBLIVION. NO
QUOTE IN THE
WORLD IS GONNA
CHANGE THAT.

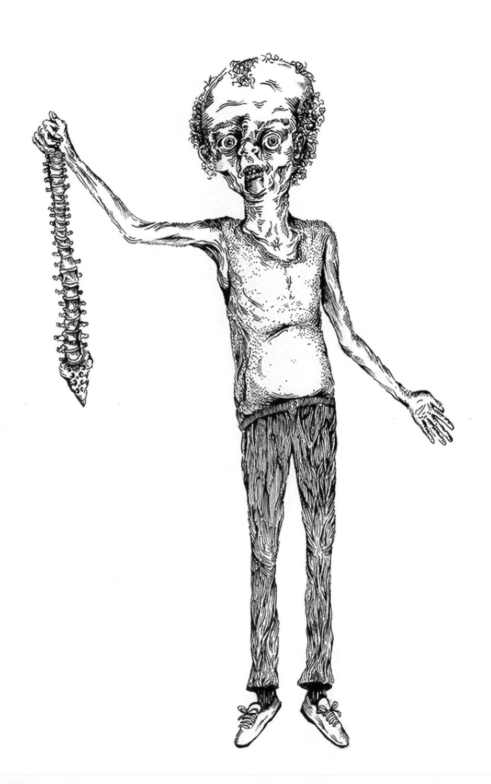

Don't
let
things
hold
you back.

JUST BE YOURSELF!
WHAT THE HELL WERE YOU THINKING?!

I want to be the
one who catches
you when you fall.

— Floor

If you're wrong 100% of the time,
you're right 0% of the time.
A wise man said that.
Spoiler: it was me.

YOU HAVE TO BE REAL
WITH YOURSELF
BEFORE YOU CAN BE
REAL WITH SOMEONE ELSE

AND YOU
REALLY SUCK.

IF YOU CAN'T
BEAT THEM,
THERE'S STILL
A GOOD CHANCE
TO ANNOY THEM.

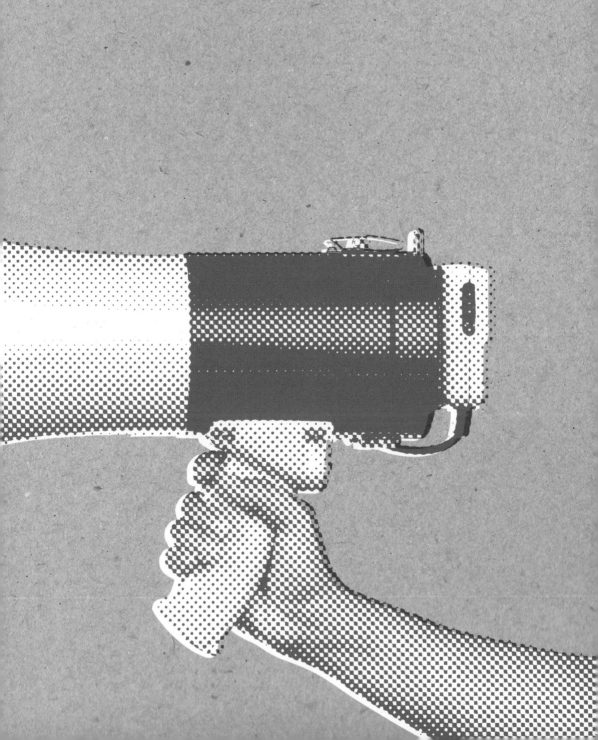

WAYS INSPIRATIONAL QUOTES ARE USED

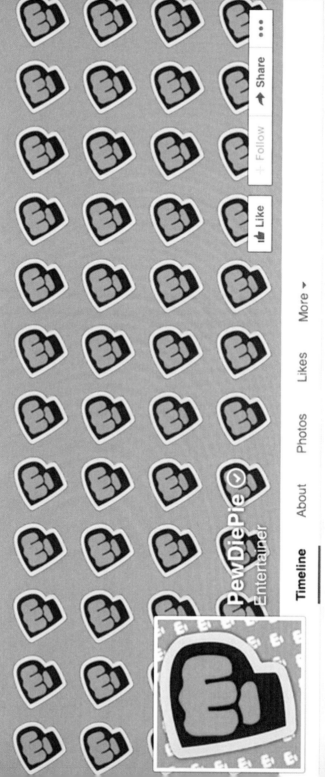

98% TO POST ON FACEBOOK TO FEEL BETTER ABOUT YOURSELF

PewDiePie ✓
Entertainer

Timeline   About   Photos   Likes   More ▾

👍 Like   ✚ Follow   ➦ Share   •••

📝 Post   🖼 Photo/Video

6.2m people like this

Invite friends to like this Page

THANKS TO THE BROS

Biggest thanks to Marzia! And big thanks to Amy and Kevin Finnerty, Sarah Wick, and everyone at Maker Studios; Alex Clarke, Ben Schrank, Casey McIntyre, Hattie Adam-Smith, Francesca Russell, Elyse Marshall, John Hamilton and his design team, Matt Carr, Susan Bell, photographer, and everyone at Penguin Books; all the bros; the pugs; and lastly to Duck.

An Imprint of Penguin Random House

Penguin.com

ISBN: 9781101999042

Printed in the United States of America

1 3 5 7 9 10 8 6 4 2

PICTURE CREDITS

Photography © Susan Bell: 5, 16, 21, 37, 44, 50–51, 54–5, 63, 71, 100–101, 120, 124–5, 132–3, 135, 140–41, 146–7, 150–51, 156–7, 166–7, 172, 177, 182–3, 194, 198–9, 213, 226–7, 236.

Grateful acknowledgement is made by the publisher for permission to reproduce the images on the following pages:

2–3 © Shutterstock; 10–11 © plainpicture/ponton and © Mary Evans/Classic Stock/H. Armstrong Roberts; 17 © Tim Hawley/Getty Images; 18–19 © Attck; 22–23 © Linda Steward/Getty Images; 25 © Viktor Flumé, © Getty Images; 26–7 © iStock.com/photka, © iStock.com/spawns; 29 © Tobi Corney/Getty Images; 39 © iStock.com/Rtimages, © iStock.com/eelnosiva; 48–9 © Sebastian Marmaduke/Image Source; 52–3; 56 © Warren Photographic; 60–61 © iStock.com/Korovin, ©iStock.com/Ridofranz, © iStock/Noppol Mahawanjam; 62 © iStock.com/egal, © iStock.com/GlobalP, © iStock.com/CoreyFord; 64–5 © iStock.com/GlobalStock; 66–7 © iStock.com/PeopleImages, © Oriontrail/ Shutterstock, © iStock.com/GlobalP, © iStock.com/camdoc3; 68 © Daniel Day/Getty Images; 70 © iStock.com/ViewApart; 74–5 © iStock.com/Nata_Slavetskaya; © iStock. com/Lambros Kazan, © iStock.com/Oksanita; 78–9; 82–3 © Sarah Lynn Paige/Getty Images, © Shebeko/Shutterstock; 86 © mikeledray/Shutterstock; 87 © Getty Images; 88 © fridhelm/Shutterstock; 90 © CSA Images/Color Printstock Collection/Getty Images; 91 © Image Source/Getty Images; 94 © fStop Images GmbH/Alamy; 95 © Victor Albrow/ Getty Images; 98–9 © iStock.com/mazzzur; 104 © Angus Hamilton; 105 © Getty Images; 107 © PM Images/Getty Images; 108–9 © Chelsea Kedron/Geety Images; 115 © Christian Adams/Getty Images; 118 © Belovodchenko Anton/Shutterstock; 119 © Image Source/ Getty Images, © Shutterstock; 123 © iStock.com/zakazpc; 126–7 © Piotr Marcinski/ Shutterstock; 129 © iStock.com/CSA-Printstock; 137 © iStock.com/vuk8691, © iStock. com/Creativeye99; 142–3 © Rtimages/Shutterstock, © urchyks/Shutterstock; 151 © Peter Dazeley/Getty Images; 152 © iStock.com/lisinski; 156–7 © Shutterstock; 160–61 © iStock. com/GlobalP, © iStock.com/kirstypargeter; 168–9 © iStock.com/jorgeantonio; 170–71 © Pawel Michalowski/Shutterstock; 174–5 © John Lund/Getty Images; 180 © Mark Murphy/ Getty Images; 184–5 © Felix Kjellberg; 190 © DEBROCKE/Corbis; 191 © Peter Dazeley/ Getty Images; 197 © chaoss/Shutterstock; 200 © Ron Levine/Getty Images, © Steve Mcsweeny/Getty Images; 201 © Shutterstock; 216 © iStock.com/Yuri_Arcurs; 218–19 © VICTOR HABBICK VISIONS/Getty Images, © Nadiia Ishchenko/Shutterstock; 222 © Angela Wyant/Getty Images; 224 © Maria Toutoudaki/Getty Image; 225 © EVERSOFINE/ Getty Images; 228 © CSA Images/Getty Images; 229 © Milena Milani/Shutterstock; 230–31 © iStock.com/manley099.

Illustration © Kevin Long: 40–41, 138–9, 220–21 and © Ian Stevenson: 14–15, 144–5, 153, 162.

Every effort has been made to attain the correct image permissions, however any omissions will be corrected in future editions.

I

LiED